Brushing Teeth

by Mari Schuh

Consulting Editor:
Gail Saunders-Smith, PhD

Consultant:
Lori Gagliardi CDA, RDA, RDH, EdD

Capstone
press
North Mankato, Minnesota

Pebble Plus is published by Capstone Press,
1710 Roe Crest Drive, North Mankato, Minnesota 56003.
www.capstonepub.com

Library of Congress Cataloging-in-Publication Data
Schuh, Mari C., 1975–
    Brushing teeth/by Mari Schuh.
    p. cm. — (Pebble plus. Healthy teeth)
    Summary: "Simple text, photographs, and diagrams present information brushing teeth properly"—
Provided by publisher.
    Includes bibliographical references and index.
    ISBN-13: 978-1-4296-1240-1 (hardcover)
    ISBN-10: 1-4296-1240-1 (hardcover)
    ISBN-13: 978-1-4296-1786-4 (softcover)
    ISBN-10: 1-4296-1786-1 (softcover)
    1. Teeth — Care and hygiene — Juvenile literature. I. Title. II. Series.
RK63.S38 2008
617.6'01 — dc22   2007027117

Editorial Credits
Sarah L. Schuette, editor; Veronica Bianchini, designer and illustrator

Photo Credits
Capstone Press/Karon Dubke, all

The author dedicates this book to her niece, Avery Schuh of Mankato, Minnesota, who has excellent
brushing habits.

Note to Parents and Teachers

The Healthy Teeth set supports national science standards related to personal health.
This book describes and illustrates brushing teeth. The images support early readers in
understanding the text. The repetition of words and phrases helps early readers learn
new words. This book also introduces early readers to subject-specific vocabulary words,
which are defined in the Glossary section. Early readers may need assistance to read some
words and to use the Table of Contents, Glossary, Read More, Internet Sites, and Index
sections of the book.

Table of Contents

Why Brush?

Luke brushes his teeth after he eats and before bed. Brushing keeps his mouth feeling fresh and clean.

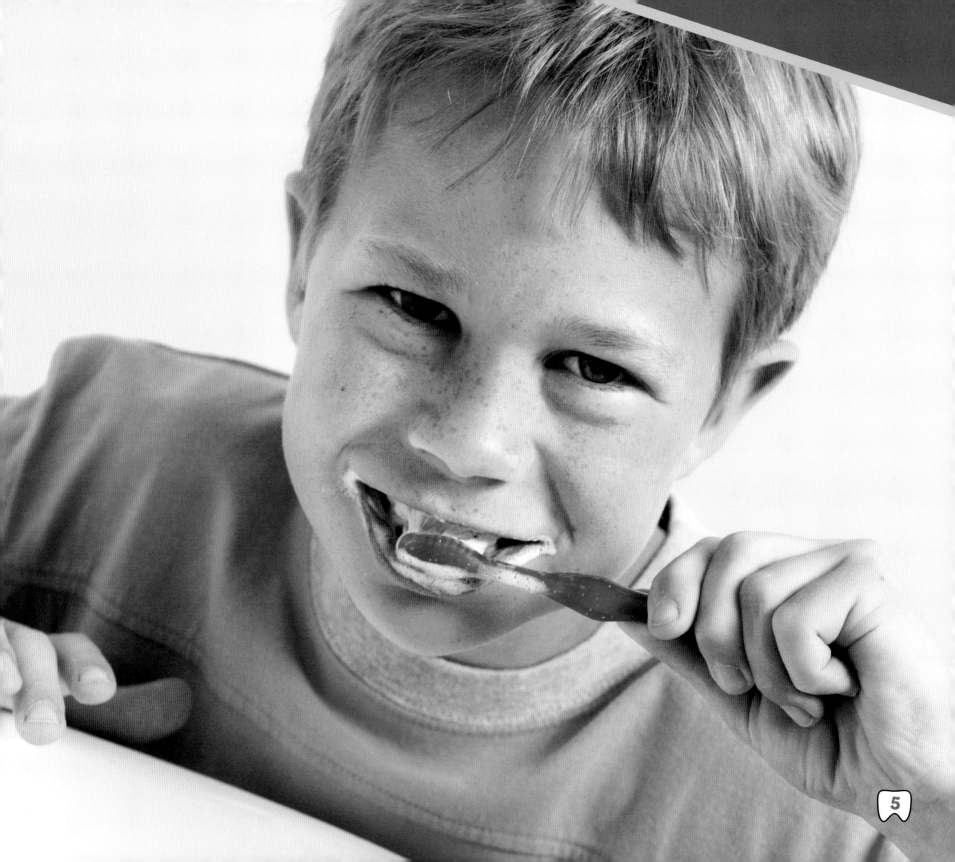

Brushing gets rid
of food and plaque.
Plaque can cause cavities.

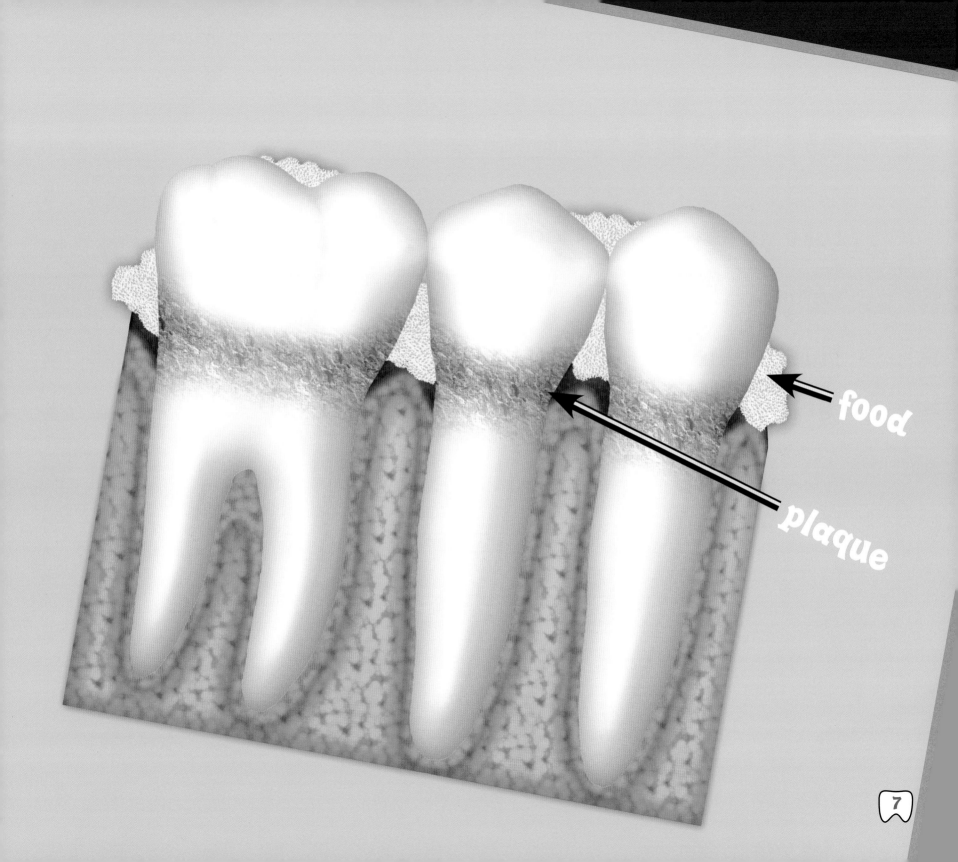

food

plaque

Brushing

Luke uses a small toothbrush with soft bristles. Fluoride toothpaste for kids is also good to use.

Luke uses a pea-sized amount
of toothpaste.
He starts by gently brushing
all sides of his teeth.

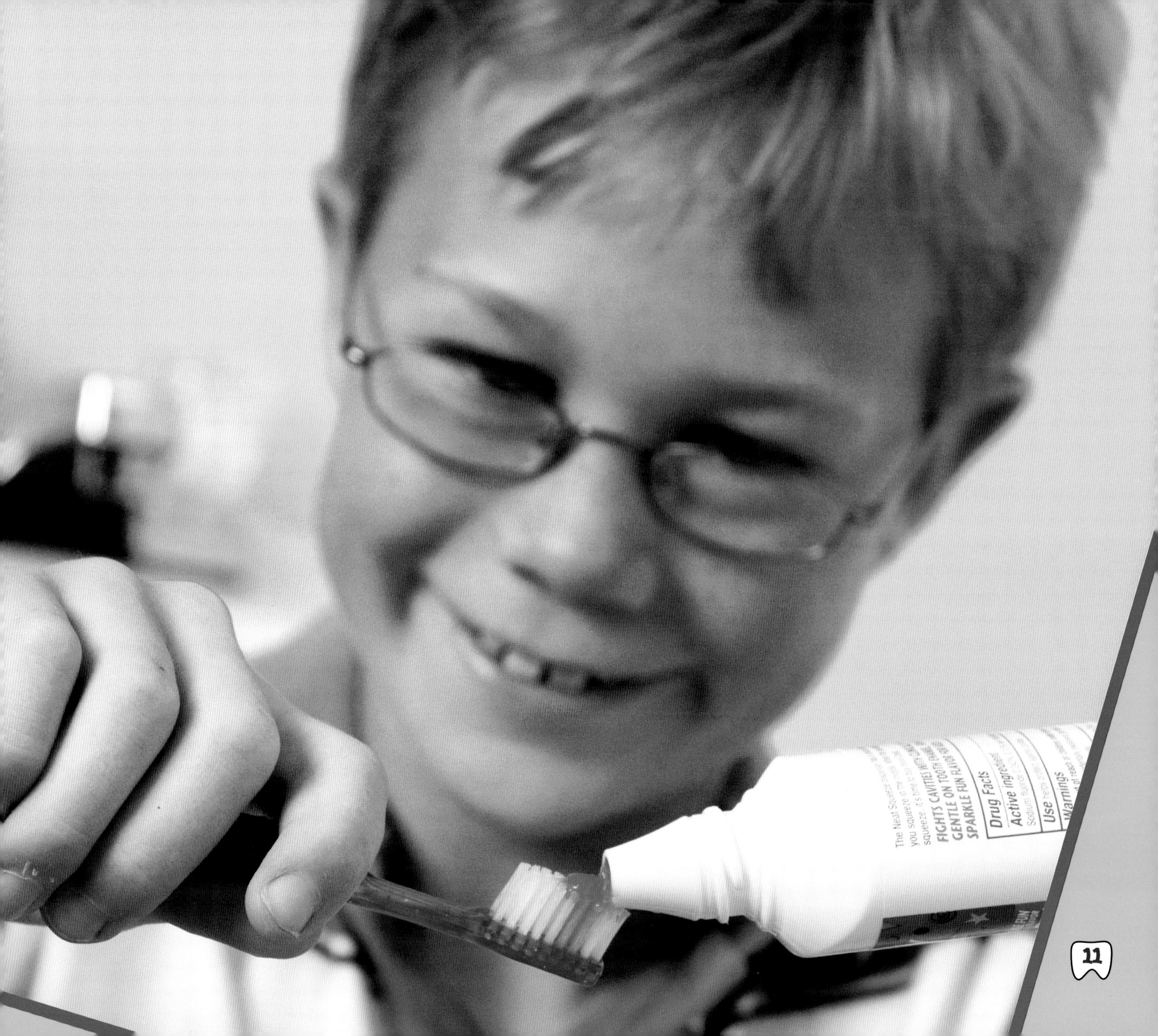
Drug Facts
Use
Warnings

Luke brushes back and forth
in small circles.
He brushes the tops of his
teeth and his tongue too.

When he's done brushing,
Luke spits out the toothpaste.
He swishes his mouth
with water.

Luke rinses out his toothbrush.

He lets it dry.

Luke never shares his
toothbrush with anyone.

17

The bristles on Luke's toothbrush get bent and worn.
He gets a new toothbrush every few months.

Healthy Teeth

Brush your teeth
at least two times a day.
You'll have a healthy smile
your whole life!

Glossary

cavity — a decayed part or hole in a tooth; brushing your teeth helps prevent cavities.

bristle — one of the short, stiff pieces on a toothbrush that look like hair

fluoride — a mineral put in many kinds of toothpaste to make enamel strong

gentle — not rough; teeth should be brushed gently; brushing teeth too hard can hurt them.

plaque — a sticky coating that forms on your teeth; plaque is made from food, germs, and saliva.

tooth — one of the white, bony parts of your mouth that you use for biting and chewing food

Read More

DeGezelle, Terri. *Taking Care of My Teeth.* Pebble Plus. Keeping Healthy. Mankato, Minn.: Capstone Press, 2006.

Gaff, Jackie. *Why Must I Brush My Teeth?* Why Must I? North Mankato, Minn.: Cherrytree Books, 2005.

Spilsbury, Louise. *Why Should I Brush My Teeth?: And Other Questions About Healthy Teeth.* Heinemann Infosearch. Chicago: Heinemann, 2003.

Internet Sites

FactHound offers a safe, fun way to find Internet sites related to this book. All of the sites on FactHound have been researched by our staff.

Here's how:

1. Visit *www.facthound.com*

2. Choose your grade level.

3. Type in this book ID **1429612401** for age-appropriate sites. You may also browse subjects by clicking on letters, or by clicking on pictures and words.

4. Click on the **Fetch It** button.

FactHound will fetch the best sites for you!

Index

Word Count: 147
Grade: 1
Early-Intervention Level: 18